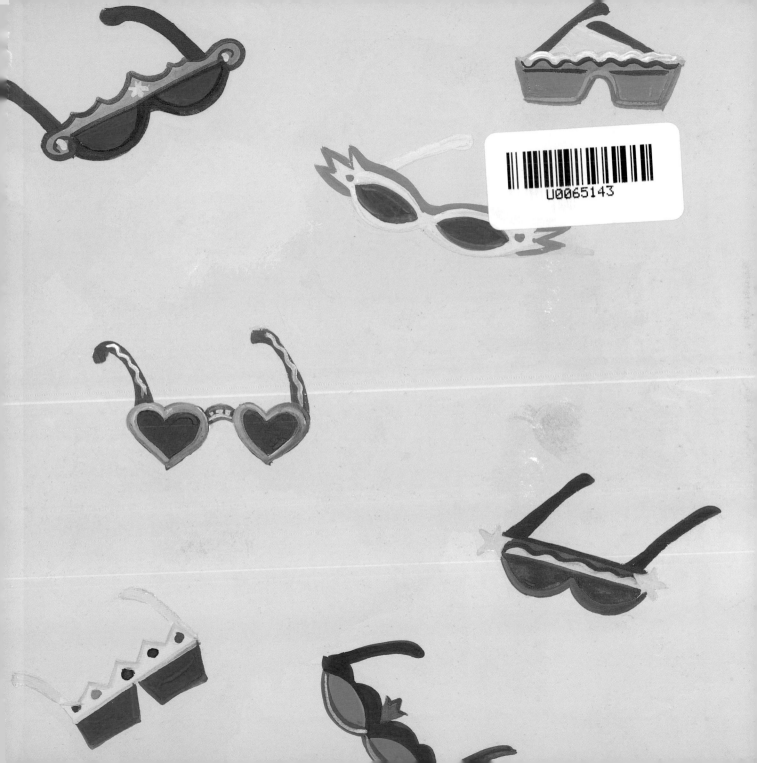

ZIPPY AND ZOE GO TO THE BEACH

by Carla Golembe

For my husband, Joe

Zippy and Zoe are going to the beach.
Zippy puts on his *swimsuit and his hat.

Zoe puts on her swimsuit and her *sunglasses.

"Let's not forget our towels and our *surfboards," says Zoe.

Zippy and Zoe get on the bus.

The bus stops at the beach.
Zippy points his *paw. "Look! It's the ocean."

They build a sand castle.

Zoe *falls asleep and Zippy *buries her in the sand.
She wakes up and pushes the sand off with her tail.
"Are you hungry?" Zippy asks.
"Oh no!" says Zoe. "We forgot to bring lunch."

All the people on the beach are eating lunch.

"I wish we had something to eat," says Zippy.

"Me too," Zoe *sighs. "Let's go surfing. If we surf we won't think about food."

They swim out into the water and wait for a wave.

Under the water they see lots of fish.
Zoe points at the fish and *licks her lips.

Zippy thinks, "Those fish look like lunch!"

He *grabs a big fish.

Back on the beach Zoe smiles, "I have a great idea." She climbs up a *coconut palm tree.
"*Watch out!" she calls to Zippy. She throws a coconut to the ground. "Fresh coconut!" she cries.

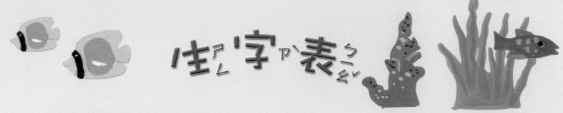

生字表

n.＝名詞，v.＝動詞

賽皮與柔依去海邊

p.3

賽皮和柔依要去海邊。
賽皮穿上他的泳衣，戴上他的帽子。

p.4

柔依穿上她的泳衣，戴上她的太陽眼鏡。

p.5

柔依說：「不要忘了帶毛巾和沖浪板喔！」

p.6

賽皮和柔依搭上了公車。

p.7

公車在海邊停下來。
賽皮用腳爪指著外面說：「你看！是海耶！」

p.8

賽皮和柔依在沙灘上鋪上毛巾。

p.9

他們跑進海裡，在波浪間玩耍。
柔依笑著說：「海浪搔得我的腳爪好癢喔！」

23

p.10

他們堆了一座沙堡。

p.11

柔依睡著了，賽皮把她的身體埋進沙子裡。
她醒來之後，用尾巴把身上的沙子推掉。
賽皮問她：「妳餓了嗎？」
柔依說：「糟了！我們忘了帶午餐了！」

p.12

沙灘上的人們全都在吃午餐。
賽皮說：「真希望我們有東西吃。」
柔依嘆了一口氣說：「我也是。我們去沖浪吧！
沖浪的時候，我們就不會想著食物了。」

p.13

他們往外游到水裡，等著海浪來。

p.14

有個海浪過來了，把他們抬了起來。柔依大
叫：「好好玩喔！」

p.15

突然間，有個更大的浪打了過來，把他們高高
托起。它把賽皮和柔依又再托得更高，直到他

們從沖浪板上掉下來。賽皮說：「唉呀！」

p.16

他們在海底看到了好多魚。柔依指著那些魚，舔了舔嘴唇。

p.17

賽皮心想：「那些魚看起來可以當作午餐！」

p.18

他抓了一條大魚。

p.19

回到沙灘上後，柔依笑著說：「我有個很棒的點子喔！」然後她爬上一棵椰子樹。
她對賽皮大喊：「小心！」接著丟了一顆椰子到地上。她大聲說：「新鮮的椰子喔！」

p.20

他們升火烤魚，在沙灘上舉行野餐。賽皮說：「好好吃喔！」

p.21

他們吃得飽飽的，躺在陽光下。賽皮說：「這真是完美的一天！」

Part. 1 故事重組

下面有六張圖片，每張圖片都有一段文字敘述，它們沒有按照順序排列。請你仔細看一看下面這六張圖片和句子，並按照故事發生的順序，在每張圖左上方填入 1～6 的號碼。 （正確答案在第 28 頁喔！）

Zippy and Zoe are hungry. But they forget their lunch!

Zippy and Zoe get on the bus. The bus stops at the beach.

Zippy grabs a fish in the water.

Zippy and Zoe go surfing.

Zippy and Zoe have a picnic on the beach.

Zippy and Zoe are going to the beach.

Part. 2

如果你要去海邊玩，你會帶什麼東西去呢？請先跟著 CD 的 Track 4，將下面物品的英文名稱唸一遍。

接著，選出你想要帶去海邊的東西，然後在圖片的右上角打勾吧！如果有人和你一起做這個活動，你們可以互相討論選出來的東西有什麼不同。

towel

swimming suit

hat

sunglasses

surfboard

beach ball

food

🐾 About the Author

Carla Golembe is the illustrator of thirteen children's books, five of which she wrote. Carla has won several awards including a New York Times Best Illustrated Picture Book Award. She has also received illustration awards from Parents' Choice and the American Folklore Society. She has twenty-five years of college teaching experience and, for the last thirteen years, has given speaker presentations and workshops to elementary schools. She lives in Southeast Florida, with her husband Joe and her cats Zippy and Zoe.

🐾 關於作者

Carla Golembe 擔任過十三本童書的繪者，其中五本是由她寫作的。Carla 曾多次獲獎，包括《紐約時報》最佳圖畫書獎。她也曾獲<u>全美父母首選基金會</u>，以及<u>美國民俗學會</u>的插畫獎項。她有二十五年的大學教學經驗，而在過去的十三年中，曾經在多所小學中演講及舉辦研討會。她目前和丈夫 Joe 以及她的貓——賽皮與柔依，住在美國佛羅里達州東南部。

賽皮與柔依系列

ZIPPY AND ZOE SERIES

想知道我們發生了什麼驚奇又爆笑的事嗎？
歡迎學習英文0-2年的小朋友一起來分享我們的故事——
「賽皮與柔依系列」，讓你在一連串有趣的事情中學英文！

精裝／附中英雙語朗讀CD／全套六本

Carla Golembe 著／繪

本局編輯部 譯

Hello！我是賽皮，我喜歡畫畫、做餅乾，還有跟柔依一起去海邊玩。偷偷告訴你們一個秘密：我在馬戲團表演過喔！

Hi，我是柔依，今年最開心的事，就是賽皮送我一張他親手畫的生日卡片！賽皮是我最要好的朋友，他很聰明也很可愛，我們兩個常常一起出去玩！

賽皮與柔依系列有：

1 賽皮與綠色顏料
(Zippy and the Green Paint)

2 賽皮與馬戲團
(Zippy and the Circus)

3 賽皮與超級大餅乾
(Zippy and the Very Big Cookie)

4 賽皮做運動
(Zippy Chooses a Sport)

5 賽皮學認字
(Zippy Reads)

6 賽皮與柔依去海邊
(Zippy and Zoe Go to the Beach)

I Love My Family Series

我愛我的家 系列

Kathleen R. Seaton　著／姚紅　繪

附中英雙語朗讀 CD

適讀對象：學習英文 0～2 年者（國小 1～3 年級適讀）

六本全新創作的中英雙語繪本，
六個溫馨幽默的故事，
帶領小朋友們進入單純可愛的小班的生活，
跟他一起分享和家人之間親密的感情！

Grandmother

Grandfather

Big Brother

Father

Mother

Ben

Little Brother

Little Sister

Big Sister

國家圖書館出版品預行編目資料

Zippy and Zoe Go to the Beach:賽皮與柔依去海邊
／ Carla Golembe著;Carla Golembe繪;本局編輯
部譯.－－初版一刷.－－臺北市：三民，2006
面；　　公分.－－(Fun心讀雙語叢書.賽皮與柔
依系列)
中英對照
ISBN 957－14－4455－3　　(精裝)
1.英國語言－讀本
523.38　　　　　　　　　　　　　　　94026569

網路書店位址　http://www.sanmin.com.tw

© **Zippy and Zoe Go to the Beach**
　　──賽皮與柔依去海邊

著作人　Carla Golembe
繪　者　Carla Golembe
譯　者　本局編輯部
發行人　劉振強
著作財
產權人　三民書局股份有限公司
　　　　臺北市復興北路386號
發行所　三民書局股份有限公司
　　　　地址／臺北市復興北路386號
　　　　電話／(02)25006600
　　　　郵撥／0009998－5
印刷所　三民書局股份有限公司
門市部　復北店／臺北市復興北路386號
　　　　重南店／臺北市重慶南路一段61號
初版一刷　2006年1月
編　號　S 806221
定　價　新臺幣壹佰捌拾元整
行政院新聞局登記證局版臺業字第○二○○號

有著作權‧不准侵害

ISBN　957－14－4455－3　　(精裝)